This book is dedicated to
my best friend and the world's greatest wife.

Linda Sue Bader

To Supplement or Not To Supplement

Copyright 1995, Dr. Myles H. Bader

ISBN: 0-9632899-5-0

Published by: Northstar Publishing Company
1818 Industrial Road, Suite 209, Las Vegas, NV 89102
1-800-717-6001

Desktop Publishing with Corel Ventura by: Suzanne Merritt-Palka
Cover Design by: Michael Lynch

Printed in the United States of America
First Printing 1995

A WORD ABOUT THE AUTHOR

Dr. Myles H. Bader (known by many as "The Doctor of Food Facts,") has been heard on over 750 radio and television talk show interviews nationwide; including The Oprah Winfrey Show, Discovery Channel's "Home Matters", The Sun Up Show, Health Quest and The Mike and Maty Show to mention only a few of his television appearances. Dr. Bader received his Doctoral Degree in Public Health with a clinical specialty in Preventive Care from Loma Linda University in California.
Lendon Smith, M.D., better known as the Good Morning America Doctor for many years has this to say of Dr. Bader, "He is highly knowledgeable in the areas of health, nutrition and preventive medicine."

Dr. Bader has practiced preventive care for 20 years in major medical clinics throughout California. He has established numerous prevention programs for Fortune 500 companies, government agencies and senior citizen organizations. He also served as the nutritional advisor for 400 Gold's Gyms internationally. Dr. Bader developed and taught numerous seminars for professionals and the general public in the areas of wellness, weight management and nutrition. Currently Dr. Bader is the Director of Preventive Medical Services at the prestigious Fremont Medical Centers in Las Vegas, Nevada.

His current book "4001 Food Facts and Chef's Secrets" is enjoying phenomenal success throughout the United States and Canada. The book is filled with over 4500 facts, tips, hints and secrets on and about food. There are facts on health and nutrition, secrets on food preparation from chef's around the world, tips on buying and storing foods, unique uses of certain foods other than eating, and thousands of tips that save you time and money in all areas of your life. Celebrity host Robin Leach says of "4001 Food Facts and Chef's Secrets", "a fun and useful book that should be on every kitchen counter in America."

Dr. Bader has recently formulated a "Breakthrough" product in the area of food preservation. Called "Oxytrol", it is an all natural food oxidation retardant, that reduces the effects of browning and will not alter the flavor of food. Simply spray on vegetables, fruits, meats and dairy products and your food stays fresher longer, naturally.

FOREWORD

Why as an intelligent nation do we continue to commit "Nutritional Suicide?" I keep asking myself this question over and over as I explore the mountains of nutrition education material, most of which is available to the public. The facts regarding how to eat better for better health are everywhere, yet we either let them go in one ear and out the other or we feel we are above it all, and that poor health habits and poor nutrition will never affect us or our children. How wrong we are, and how little most Americans really know about nutrition.

We purchase foods that are grown in nutrient depleted soils, foods that lack the basic nutrition we are purchasing them for. We are eating a diet consisting of chemicals and additives, the effect of which is largely unknown.

Our beef comes from cattle that are hormonized to make them grow faster, then nitrited to make them retain their nice red color. We allow our children to eat sugar-coated cereals because we're afraid they may not eat breakfast. We drink gallons of caffeinated beverages each year to stimulate us and keep us awake, then take sleeping pills to put us to sleep.

We are a nation of people who have forgotten how to eat right. We rely too much on convenience foods and fast-food restaurants. Remember, you and you alone are responsible for your family's health.

This book is light, easy reading and a very practical guide to nutrition. It serves as an eye opener and hopefully will stimulate your interest in gaining knowledge you should have regarding the food you're putting into the only body God's going to give you.

Lendon Smith, M.D.

Table of Contents

THE BASICS

This booklet has been written to try to enlighten every person to the wonderful world of optimum health, a state of being that few of you will ever reach unless you become more aware of the true miracle of life and how the human body functions. We must learn how to protect our health, ourselves, and not depend on someone else to do it for us.

We are presently existing in an environment that is becoming more and more hostile to our health. Unless we learn more about this new environment and how to cope with it, our health will deteriorate and disease processes will continue to grasp a foothold and shorten our lifespans.

THE DELICATE BALANCE

We are all composed of minerals, water, proteins, fats and carbohydrates. We run by a series of biochemical reactions, the likes of which would make a computer stand up and take notice. These biochemical reactions take place in thousandths of a second and trillions of times per minute.

The complexities of the human body are so complicated that they may never be fully understood by medical science. The mysteries are endless and disease processes can gain a foothold if only one of the trillions of cells does not have the raw materials it needs or is damaged.

Many people feel that they are giving their bodies all the proper raw materials it needs, and maybe they are; however, even if we ate all the perfect foods in the exact right proportions, there are environmental factors that are above and beyond our control that can cause the healthiest body to react unfavorably and thus lead to a disease process gaining a foothold.

THE CELL

When discussing health and trying to obtain optimum health, it is necessary to say a few words about the cell. We are basically composed of approximately 300 trillion cells or, if it's easier, 500 billion cells per pound in an average 150-pound adult. Millions of cells die each day and about 1 million new cells are born each and every hour of every day.

If your over your ideal weight, just think of all those extra billions of cells you have to feed and care for. An example of the complexity of the cellular activities may be better understood by realizing that one liver cell may contain at least 1000 enzymes to assist and speed along reactions which occur at the rate of 1000 times per second.

The cell is responsible for everything that goes on in the body, it all starts at the cellular level. There are small "organelles" that produce energy, another that manufactures proteins and others that store the raw materials and supply them when needed. The cell is surrounded by a very complex membrane cell wall which is selective and only allows certain nutrients to enter and specific manufactured products to leave for transport all over the body.

Cancer cells, for instance, may start by having a poor cell wall, possibly one that was not able to obtain the quality raw material it needed to make a healthy cell wall. A poor cell wall is more subject to damage by a free-radical molecule, which will be discussed in another chapter.

The cell also has a very sensitive potassium/sodium balance which is upset by consuming too many refined/processed foods, which increase the sodium and throw the balance off. When this happens the cell is unable to clear the toxins properly and may become diseased.

A NEW YOU

Cells don't live forever! They are continually replicating themselves and making new cells. This means that you are continually replacing the old worn-out cells with fresh new cells. The importance of this most of us never really think about, but you are actually replacing yourself, slowly but surely.

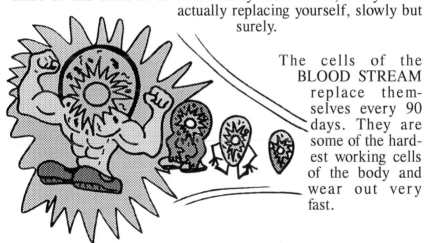

The cells of the BLOOD STREAM replace themselves every 90 days. They are some of the hardest working cells of the body and wear out very fast.

The cells of the SOFT TISSUES replace themselves every 3 years. This means that all your organs are new every 3 years, depending on their cycle.

The cells of the HARD TISSUES replace themselves every 7 years. These include your bones.

The nutrient needs of the cell vary from person to person so widely that it is impossible to advise a person what the "perfect" diet is for them. No two people are identical, therefore their nutrient needs are different. Some may be under more stress, exercise more, live in a smoggy city, smoke cigarettes, etc. Lifestyles vary

3

and so do the nutrient needs of the cell, especially if they are to function at their optimum level.

However, keep in mind one very important factor!

The cell is very adaptive and if the only nutrients available are poor-quality nutrients, the cell may still use them and make a poor quality new cell. In order to survive it has to have a steady supply of nutrients, raw materials.

What all this may mean is that if you start now with a good diet, take the proper supplements, and do everything you can to have a good overall lifestyle, you will be a "better you" in approximately 7 years. It doesn't happen overnight, which is why many people get frustrated when starting a healthy lifestyle regimen, especially when a supplement program is involved. BE PATIENT AND LET NATURE TAKE ITS COURSE.

LET'S MAKE A NEW YOU!

Every 90 days the blood cells renew

Every 3 years the soft tissues renew

Every 7 years the hard tissue renews

THE QUALITY OF THE NEW YOU DEPENDS ON:

- The condition of the walls of the small intestines.

- Nutrient bioavailability.

- The quality and quantity of the foods we eat.

- The quality and type of supplements we take.

- The number of factors that affect our biochemical efficiency.

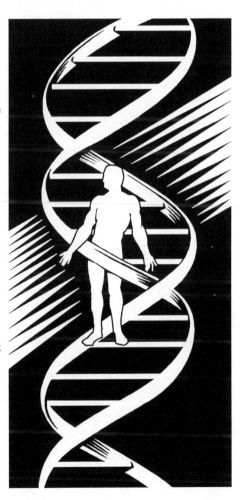

BIOAVAILABILITY

WHAT DOES IT MEAN, WHY IS IT SO IMPORTANT?

To put it simply, it is the relative rate (or speed) at which a supplement or drug reaches the general circulation. When you take a supplement orally there are numerous factors that may affect the amount of the active product that actually will be available for utilization by the cells. The factors include:

1. Quality control during the manufacture and formulation processes.

2. Solubility, or how fast it will dissolve in the stomach.

3. Tablet size.

4. Dietary patterns.

5. Whether the minerals are "chelated."

6. The type of sustained release system.

SCRUB-A-DUB-DUB

The body in its effort to cleanse itself of foreign materials that may cause damage is able to produce an enzyme called Lipoprotein Lipase (LPL). This enzyme is released from specialized cells in the walls of the artery and acts as a cleaning agent to remove unwanted debris.

This debris accumulates on the walls of the arteries and may be one of the causes of plaque build-up leading to an eventual closure of the artery causing a heart attack or stroke. It can also make an already-existing problem more serious.

Antioxidants, especially vitamin C, stimulates the production of LPL. Since most diets are deficient in vitamin C and we are continually bombarded by numerous environmental factors that contribute to our reduction of vitamin C stores, we may not consume enough to cover all needs. Supplementation is a must.

Studies in the future may implicate the lack of adequate LPL as one of the significant causes of arteriosclerosis and hardening of the arteries.

INNER POLLUTION

NUTRIENTS NIGHTMARE

Let's have some fun and follow some nutrients from the time you consume them to the time they arrive at the cell. This can either be a "pleasant experience" for them or a "real nightmare."

The "pleasant experience" needs little explanation. The nutrients are broken down properly, after you have chewed your food well to allow more of the foods surfaces to come in contact with the enzymes and acids that will break them down. Your intestinal tract is clean, the support system is waiting to carry the nutrients to the cell, they do their job and the cell accepts them and makes a new healthy cell.

However, to be more realistic, let's take a look at what really happens to the majority of all people. Let's take a person who has just made a decision to eat a healthy diet and start a supplement program.

They consume a balanced healthy diet with foods from all the food groups and take a quality supplement. That ends the good part of their story.

To start with, the food is not properly chewed, placing a burden on the enzymes and acids to try to reach all the surfaces needed to start the break down of the foods into their smaller components. Without this first step, a percentage of the good food will rot in the intestinal tract and never be utilized.

A percentage of the food, however, is able to be broken down and leaves the stomach and duodenum and heads for the small intestines where it hopes to be chosen for transport to the cell for utilization. As the nutrients enter the small intestines, they are

7

expecting to come into contact with the single layer of cells that line the wall of the intestines which secrete enzymes to further breakdown the nutrients into their very small component parts; however, the cells are blocked by a black slimy, gooey encrustation and only a small percentage of them are broken down.

The person ate a good meal and the cells never received their quality nutrients in an adequate supply. This happens day in and day out to most people. Even taking handfuls of supplements can't solve this problem. Intestinal cleansing will!

While the above is an oversimplification of the problems that exist in the intestinal tract, the following will explain in more depth what really occurs:

1. The food arrives in the small intestines partially broken down. Specialized cells secrete a special mucous which lines and protects the walls before the liver, pancreas and gall bladder add digestive juices and enzymes into the intestinal tract.

2. The cells that line the intestines secrete enzymes that break the nutrients into their smallest components. These cells are the most amazing of all. They recognize the nutrients needed by the body and absorb just enough of them to nourish the cells. Every nutrient that enters the body must traverse these cells.

3. In a healthy body 90% of the carbohydrates, fats, proteins and supplements that pass through the intestinal tract are reduced into sugar, glycerol, fatty acids, basic supplemental and mineral components and amino acids.

4. Problems occur when the walls of the intestines become encrusted with dried fecal material that was never sent to the colon, and residues of undigested foodstuffs. These act as a blocking agent and the small cilia attached to the nutrient- selective cells are unable to trap the nutrients as they pass by.

Problems can also occur in the colon from residues of undigested foods entering from the small intestines. These problems can cause a complete backup of the transit system, leading to poor elimination of toxic materials.

As undigested foodstuffs and the resulting fecal material remain in the colon, more fluids are drawn from them, thus making it more difficult to eliminate them. Poor transit times through the colon are responsible for a variety of problems, most of which could be avoided by having a clean system and a program of regular intestinal cleansing.

The following are a few of the possible problems:

1. Stretching of the colon walls by old material and its accumulation, causing mechanical abnormalities.

2. Surrounding structures are affected due to malformation of pouch-like structures.

3. Pressure is created on the abdomen.

4. Prolapsed Colon - Drooping or sagging of the transverse colon.

5. Collapsed Colon - One or more sacs close in on themselves.

6. Redundant Colon - Folds back on itself.

7. Diverticulosis - Inflamed outpouchings.

8. Hemorrhoids - Swelling of varicose veins.

9. Constipation - Overly packed feces or old hardened fecal material stuck to the walls.

The end result may be what is called "autointoxication" or simply the body poisoning itself by maintaining a cesspool of decaying matter in the intestinal tract. These toxins get into the bloodstream and can poison all areas of the body, leading to illnesses.

Food transit times for a healthy person should be approximately 24 to 48 hours, not the 65 to 100 hours most of us take. The shorter times will be noticeable after a cleansing program.

NATURAL POLLUTION CONTROL

Herbal cleansing is one of the most effective methods of removing "intestinal sludge" from the intestinal tract. Quality products found on the market should contain one or more of the following natural herbs or ingredients:

Flax Seed, Bladderwrack, Oatstraw, Psyllium Seed, Burdock Root, Licorice Root, Cascara Sagrada, Buchu, Leaf, Sasparilla, Spearmint and especially Hyssop.

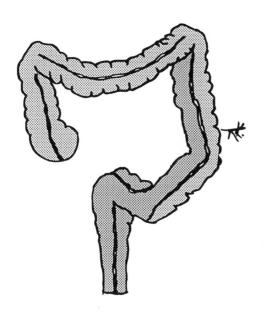

**Normal
Colon**

Improperly
working
bowels may
cause most
of the
health
problems on
the face of
the earth.

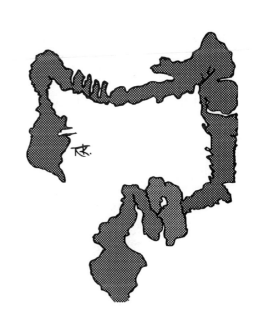

FREE RADICALS

Your tissues are made up of very small particles of matter called atoms. These atoms combine to form molecules, which contain electrically charged particles called "electrons." Electrons usually are found in pairs which provides them with their stability; however, when an electron is lost either due to outside influences or just by normal cellular metabolism, an abnormal molecule called a "free radical" is born.

Free radicals can therefore be a product of normal biochemical reactions in the body. They are not needed by the body and must be destroyed and eliminated before they cause damage to healthy cells by reacting with and actually removing the essential fatty acids from the cell wall. A free radical will literally react with anything in its path, leaving a trail of "cellular garbage" or lipofuscin pigments. It is the accumulation of these pigments that may be a significant factor in the aging process.

This free radical problem may affect all body systems including the immune system, thus reducing its effectiveness to produce antibodies to fight diseases. Free radicals may reduce the quantity of tissues that produce these antibodies, thereby lowering the overall immune system efficiency and subsequently reducing disease resistance.

Free radicals may also be implicated in reducing overall energy production by the body. Nutrients are burned in the presence of oxygen to produce energy. The exact location of this process is in the mitochondria, an area of the cell that is very high in unsaturated fatty acids which are easily damaged by the free radicals. This causes a reduction in total cellular energy output. By one estimate, each cell is hit by 10,000 free radicals every day.

FREE RADICALS....   can cause an abnormal cell to be produced.

FREE RADICALS....   can destroy the body's ability to produce the natural anti-clotting hormone PGI2.

FREE RADICALS.... have been implicated in studies as contributing to the onset and seriousness of arthritis.

FREE RADICALS.... may cause tissues to become stiff and brittle and accelerate the aging process.

FREE RADICALS.... may cause buildup of pigments or liver spots.

FREE RADICALS.... effects the integrity of collagen connective tissue which forms approximately 30% of body protein.

FREE RADICALS.... are very easily formed even when you grind meat and expose the surfaces of the smaller pieces.

THE LIST IS ENDLESS, I HOPE YOU GET THE IDEA!

FORMATION OF FREE RADICALS

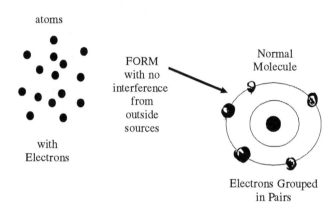

atoms

FORM
with no
interference
from
outside
sources

Normal
Molecule

with
Electrons

Electrons Grouped
in Pairs

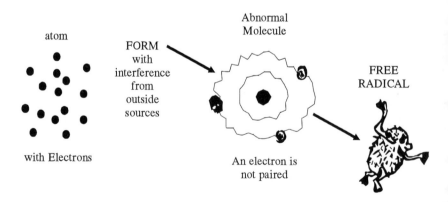

atom

FORM
with
interference
from
outside
sources

Abnormal
Molecule

FREE
RADICAL

with Electrons

An electron is
not paired

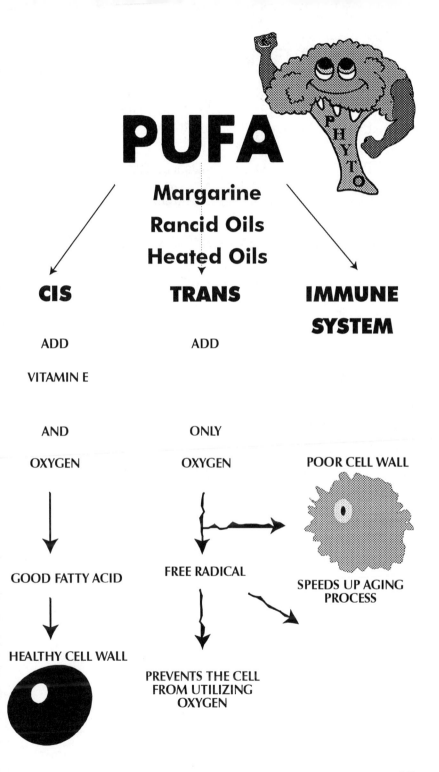

PUFA

Margarine
Rancid Oils
Heated Oils

CIS   **TRANS**   **IMMUNE SYSTEM**

ADD   ADD

VITAMIN E

AND   ONLY

OXYGEN   OXYGEN   POOR CELL WALL

GOOD FATTY ACID   FREE RADICAL

SPEEDS UP AGING PROCESS

HEALTHY CELL WALL

PREVENTS THE CELL FROM UTILIZING OXYGEN

OUR LIMITED DEFENSES

Needless to say, if all the free radicals produced in the body alone were free to do their destructive deeds uncontrolled, we would be left in a state of disease that we could never recover from.

The body, however, produces substances that fight free radicals before they can do their damage. The two most important ones are Superoxide Dimutase SOD and Glutathione Peroxidase GP.

WITHOUT THESE ENZYMES YOU WOULD QUICKLY DIE

Cancer is thought to be caused by free radicals that are not being controlled adequately and subsequently cause changes in the nucleic acids DNA and RNA.

NUTRIENTS BLOCKED FROM A CELL BY BLOCKING FACTORS

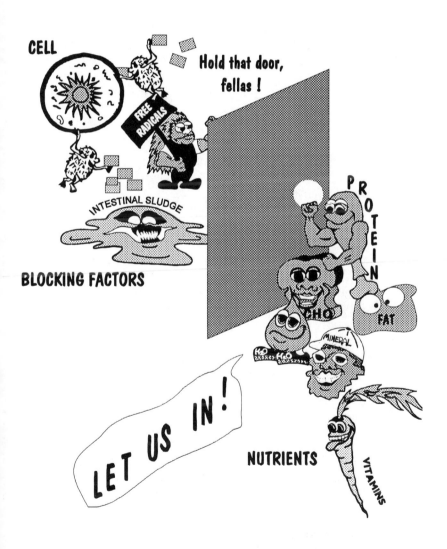

ADDING FUEL TO THE FIRE

Our bodies make free radicals and our bodies have developed defense systems to fight free radicals, but what if we flood our bodies with outside sources of free radicals: can they handle the increased load?

It is very doubtful that any person is able to produce enough free radicals fighters to handle the bombardment of free radicals produced by our current technological advances, which utilize chemicals that are detrimental to us and produce excessive free radicals.

The following list gives a number of environmental causes and discusses some of the internal and nutritional causes for free radical production:

1. CONSTIPATION   The putrefaction of waste materials and bile salts in the colon has a tendency, when left for prolonged periods of time, to produce the chemical 3-methylcholanthrene which is a free radical.

2. HEATED FATS   All fats, whether good ones or bad ones, produce trans-fatty acids which assist in the production of free radicals. The best polyunsaturated fat, cold-pressed olive oil, when heated produces trans-fatty acids. The more the oil is heated and the higher the temperature, the more trans-fatty acids are produced.

    The cell requires a quality polyunsaturated oil (PUFA) to make a healthy cell wall and prefer the good form or "cis" form.

    Processing alone results in trans-fatty acids being present in fresh store-bought products such as pure vegetable oils, which may contain up to 5% trans-acids, margarines up to 54% and shortenings up to 58%. When you heat any of these oils or products containing oil these percentages increase.

    Fats should be used in moderation, all fats! Butter may be substituted for margarine if it is unsalted and the soft variety and if you consume no more than 1 pat per day. Margarine should be of the softest type sold, which will reduce the amount of hydrogenation which adds water to increase the fat saturation content.

3. CIGARETTE SMOKE   Cadmium and tars are the most guilty, but carbon monoxide and nitrogen oxide also contribute to the biochemical chain reaction that eventually leads to free radical production.

4. CLEANING FLUIDS   The carbon tetrachloride used in many dry cleaning plants and in the home can produce gases that increase free radical production.

5. NITRITE   This chemical is used in all processed meats (hot dogs, lunch meats, bacon, sausage, etc.) to prevent the growth of ultra toxin-producing botulism organisms and carcinogen-producing aspergillus flavis mold. However, in preventing one problem this chemical can be transformed into a carcinogen called a "nitrosamine."

However, this chemical can be neutralized by having adequate levels of vitamin C in the bloodstream when it is consumed.

6. PRESERVATIVES   Many artificial preservatives, coloring agents and additives contain substances which are suspect, may produce free radicals in the body and may be removed from the market. Most people consume 6-9 pounds of these substances every year. Hope you have a healthy liver to handle all these toxins and an adequate supply of nutrients to break them down and destroy them.

7. WATER   Drinking large quantities of chlorinated water may contain hypochlorites, a free radical. Excess chlorine also causes the production of chloroform, another free radical.

8. VIRUSES   These invade the cell and may alter the functioning of the cell, thus allowing a free radical to gain a foothold.

9. ALCOHOLIC BEVERAGES   When alcohol is broken down by the body, one of the byproducts of the biochemical reaction is acetaldehyde which can produce free radicals.

10 . HYGIENE PRODUCTS   Deodorants, shampoos, toothpaste tubes and antacids are some of the products that still contain aluminum. This can build up and create a toxic environment which lends itself to free radical production.

11. FERTILIZERS   There are still many fertilizers in use today that are considered borderline and may cause free radical production in the body. Potato skins have been found to contain residues even after washing and cooking.

12. WINE BOTTLE CAPS   Many are still sealed with a lead cap and unless precautions are taken when the bottle is opened, there is the possibility of lead entering the wine.

13. HOME AND INDUSTRY FUELS   Sulphur dioxide is produced by burning fuels containing sulphur. The most guilty are coal and fuel oil. Radioactive heavy metals such as radon, thorium, radium and polonium can be generated from coal burning plants.

14. COMMON HOUSEHOLD ITEMS   felt tip markers, glues, paints, corrective fluids, and smoked fish allow hydrocarbons into the air. We inhale them and they produce free radicals in the body. Smoked foods contain hydrocarbons from the smoking process.

15. RADON GAS   A radioactive heavy metal that generates a gas that tends to seep through the ground in various parts of the United States. An active free radical producer.

16. POLYCHLORONATED BIPHENYLS (PCB's)   An industrial chemical used in pesticides, electrical wiring and hundreds of other items. Approximately 4000 tons per year have been escaping into the water supplies of the United States. They have also been found in our meats, milk and fish. Excellent carcinogen and free radical producer.

20

17. AIR POLLUTION AND SMOG   Generates   numerous hydrocarbons and heavy metals. Almost every major city in the United States has some degree of photochemical smog.

18. BENZOPYRENES   When wood or charcoal is burned the chemical benzopyrene is released, a potent carcinogen and free radical producer. When barbecuing it would be wise to scrape off any charred or blackened areas of the food. If fish or chicken are barbecued, the skin should be discarded. Consuming a charcoaled steak and not scraping the black material off is the equivalent of smoking 15 cigarettes.

19. COOKWARE   Problems may occur from cookware containing iron, copper, aluminum or non-stick surfaces. When any utensil scratches these surfaces they may release a small amount of these substances. Over time they may build up in the body and cause internal damage. Glass cookware is recommended.

20. CHEWING TOBACCO   Many harmful toxins are directly released into the bloodstream since the area under the tongue is very vascular. Most of these toxins are free radical producers.

21. FISH/SHELLFISH   High copper levels tend to help a melanoma produce more energy, and thus grow faster. Best to reduce consumption of foods high in copper such as lobster, shrimp, mussels, clams and oysters. Scallops are not too high. Pesticide residues are showing up more frequently in seafood and many are free radical producers.

22. VEHICLE FUELS   Lead and hydrocarbons from vehicle fuels are still one of the most dangerous sources of free radicals and general body poisoning.

23. CANNED FOODS   The seams on many canned foods, including baby foods, may still contain lead which may leach into the food.

24. INDUSTRIAL AND PLASTICS PRODUCTION   200 million tons of gases and particulate matter is released for us to inhale each year. A free radical breeding ground.

25. RADIATION/X-RAYS   X-rays have the ability to alter molecules and thus produce free radicals. If the tissues being irradiated have high levels of PUFA they are even more susceptible and may develop skin cancer when exposed to direct sunlight.

A study by Dr. John Gofman at UCLA showed that repeated x-rays could cause breast cancer and increased the risk of leukemia. His recommendation was to have no x-rays unless absolutely necessary.

26. AFLATOXINS   Nuts, seeds and grains that have the slightest hint of mold may contain aspergillus which readily develops into a carcinogen called aflatoxin. Inspect any packaged shelled nuts, especially if imported.

27. OZONE   Tanning booths produce ozone which are excellent free radical producers. Ozone is a strong oxidizing agent found in all polluted air. Pine trees produce ozone and free radicals by releasing hydrocarbons which interact with the air and ultraviolet light.

The Blue Ridge Mountains and the Great Smoky Mountains had a photochemical smog before the white man arrived in this country. Even Los Angeles had smog before it was settled.

Sunlight reacting with auto emissions is one of our present causes of high levels. Ozone tends to stay close to the ground and does not dissipate upwards like some of the other gases.

28. EXERCISE   Over exercising may suppress the immune system, leading to the production of free radicals.

ANTIOXIDANTS LEADING NUTRIENTS TO VICTORY OVER FREE RADICALS

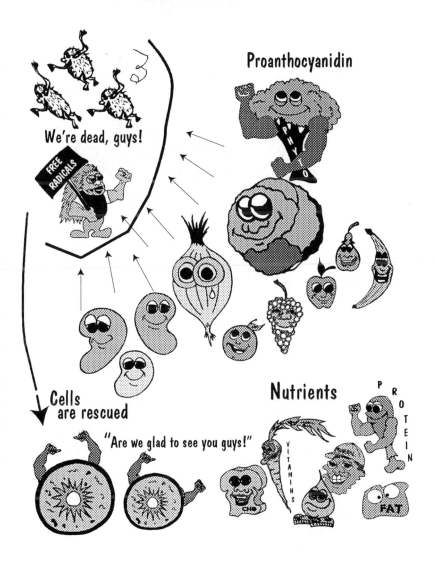

FACTORS AND ENVIRONMENTAL EFFECTS LEADING TO FREE RADICAL PRODUCTION

Constipation
Heated Fats
Cigarette Smoke
Cleaning Fluids
Nitrates
Preservatives
Water
Viruses
Alcohol
Deodorants
Fertilizers
Wine-Bottle Caps
Home and Industry Fuels
Felt Tip Markers
Paints
Radon Gas
Pcb's
Air Polution
Benzopyrenes
Cookware

Chewing Tobacco
Fish/shellfish
Toothpaste
Shampoos
Vehicle Fuels
Pesticides
Canned Foods
Corrective Fluids
Glues

Plastics Production
Radiation/x-rays
Aflatoxins
Tanning Booths
Aldehydes
Lead
Dry Cleaning
Stress
Computer Video Displays
Insulation
Sunlight/UV Rays
Smoked Foods
Emphysema
Ozone
Antacids
Furnaces/engines
Exercise
Acetaldehyde

ANTIOXIDANTS

BRING ON THE CAVALRY

Free radicals do much of their damage by "oxidizing" or, in plain English, zapping a healthy cell and either altering it permanently or killing it completely. An "antioxidant" does what it says it is, it's "anti" or "fighting against" free radicals in a search-and-destroy manner.

It is a chemical, vitamin or mineral, which tends to attach to free radicals and envelop it making them easier for the body to eliminate or neutralizing them during a stage when they appear in a biochemical reaction. Certain molecules and cellular components are more susceptible to free radical damage than others. These include DNA, RNA, lipids, fats and proteins.

The role of the antioxidants is still under investigation by numerous prestigious medical schools and universities and their effectiveness has not yet been determined. However, in all studies to date they are highly recommended in over 60 diseases as a preventative measure or to reduce the severity of a disease in patients who already show symptoms.

THE FOLLOWING ARE A FEW OF THE MORE IMPORTANT ANTIOXIDANTS

1. PROANTHOCYANIDIN   A powerful antioxidant, developed in France where it has been marketed for many years. Presently it is extracted from either grape seed or pine bark and is stated to be approximately 20% more effective than vitamin C.

    Studies are continuing on this extract and solid results should be forthcoming soon, which should show that this antioxidant is one of the most effective of all.

2. VITAMIN A (BETA CAROTENE)   Best to purchase a product that uses beta carotene as at least a percentage of its vitamin A content. Beta carotene will produce vitamin A in the body without any toxic effects and chances of an overdose.

Vitamin A improves the efficiency of the immune system as well as protecting DNA from free radicals. It also promotes the utilization of cholesterol, thus possibly assisting the body to reduce levels in the blood.

Recent studies by the National Cancer Institute have shown that levels of vitamin A suppresses an oncogene, which is thought to cause cancer, once triggered.

3. VITAMIN C   One of the most powerful antioxidants in the vitamin group. It has the ability to protect against free radicals forming, as well as providing protection for vitamins A and E from premature destruction.

Studies have shown that vitamin C strengthens and increases the effectiveness of the immune system, has a protective role in numerous cancer conditions, and aids in the assimilation of many minerals. Every cell requires vitamin C in its basic continuous metabolic process.

4. VITAMIN E   Protects the PUFA from becoming a free radical by combining with the PUFA and providing a healthy fatty acid. This process provides adequate cellular building blocks to produce strong cellular membranes, thus reducing susceptibility to foreign invaders. It neutralizes a potent chemical called a nitrosamine, as well as assisting in preventing abnormal blood clots.

Additional research has shown that vitamin E is effective in lowering cholesterol levels, reducing the incidence of tumors, enhancing the immune system capabilities and slowing the aging process in laboratory animals.

5. SELENIUM   Effective in hindering free radical damage. It is able to substitute for vitamin E in some reactions. Studies have shown that persons residing in and consuming foods grown in areas containing high selenium-content soils, are less susceptible to cardiovascular disease and cancer. Selenium also strengthens the immune system as well as being a potent anti-cancer agent in some laboratory animals.

A number of other vitamins and minerals, especially zinc, are known to have antioxidant effects; however, only the more significant ones have been mentioned.

WHY WE NEED TO SUPPLEMENT

CAUSES

Food Processing

Cooking Methods

Aging Process

Depleted Soil Minerals

Medications

Malabsorption

Smog

Smoking

Alcohol

Stress

Artificial Ingredients

Lack of Enzymes

Unbalanced Diets

Birth Control Pills

Bioavailability

Sugar Intake

Dieting

Restaurants

Sickness

Fertilizers

Storage

SUPPLEMENTATION

DO WE REALLY NEED IT?

How often have we heard that if we eat a balanced diet with all the food groups in the right proportions we will be able to obtain all the necessary nutrients our bodies need? I for one am really tired of listening to this statement, which does not take into consideration any of the following information.

Every week on television there seems to be another show telling of another problem with our food supply. We are not inspecting our foods properly due to the lack of inspectors. Our fruits and vegetables are grown in soils that are nutrient-deficient due to the depletion of trace minerals from over production.

Our products are stored too long before sale and many of the natural nutrients are processed out before they reach us. No one will ever convince me that they are enriching our foods to the level that the nutrients were originally.

We use preservatives and coloring agents that are borderline healthy and many have been proven to cause cancer in laboratory animals. We don't have time to eat a balanced diet and we kill off all the enzymes with heat before we eat the food.

Then we take a supplement that has probably lost a percentage of its potency and has a low level of "biologic activity." It is better to pay a few dollars more and purchase a high quality vitamin product with a high level of "biologic activity," than to try to save a few dollars. Many vitamin products are just not that active in providing you with a quality level of the nutrient you are buying them for.

The following information will give some insight into the "real" world of nutrition and the many factors that relate to your obtaining the level of nutrients from the foods you purchase. It will also provide additional information regarding the need for additional supplementation in relation to a variety of lifestyle factors.

PROCESSING OF FOODS

EXPOSURE TO HEAT

1. FRIED FOODS The longer the food is fried and the higher the temperature the more vitamin and mineral potency loss. Frying temperatures usually reach 375° F. Corn or safflower oils are best because of their higher smoke points of 450° F to 500° F.

2. CANNED FOODS Vitamin and mineral potency losses occur from blanching, and the sterilization process, which involve temperatures of 240° F or higher for 25-40 minutes.

3. FROZEN FOODS Many are cooked before freezing. Higher quality foods are sold fresh. Lower-quality are used in frozen foods.

4. DEHYDRATED FOODS Very dependent on the quality of the product processed. Certain methods of commercial dehydration use temperatures of 300° F.

5. DAIRY PRODUCTS Many vitamins lose their potency or are totally destroyed by the pasteurization process. The homogenization process breaks down the normal-sized fat particles, thus allowing the formation of an enzyme called "xanthine oxidase." This enzyme then enters the bloodstream and may destroy vital body chemicals that would ordinarily provide protection for the coronary arteries.

NOTE: Various nutrients have different degrees of stability under the conditions of processing and preparation. Vitamin

A is easily destroyed by heat and light. Vitamin C is not only affected by heat but is also affected by contact with certain metals such as bronze, brass, copper, cold rolled steel, or black-iron processing equipment. Studies conducted on the canning of fools found that peas and beans lose 75% of certain B vitamins, and tomatoes lose 80% of their naturally occurring zinc content.

EXPOSURE TO COLD

FROZEN FOODS   Freezing may have only minimal effect on the vitamin and mineral potency, depending on the method used and whether they are frozen shortly after being harvested. Remember, in most instances the higher quality foods are sold fresh.

FRESH FRUITS AND VEGETABLES   Sometimes   harvested before they are ripe, then allowed to ripen on the way to market. This may cause a reduction of some trace minerals.

METHODS OF FREEZING

There are four major methods of freezing foods commercially:

AIR BLAST FREEZING   Products are frozen by high velocity cold air. This is the most widely used freezing technique in the prepared food industry, and is used on all kinds of products.

PLATE FREEZING   The product is placed in contact with cold metal surfaces.

CRYOGENIC FREEZING   Freezing at very low temperatures (below minus $100°$ F) in direct contact with liquid nitrogen or carbon dioxide. Used for freezing meat patties and other meat products.

FREON IMMERSION FREEZING   Utilizes freon to freeze the product instantaneously, thus allowing the product to retain its total weight. Presently being used to freeze hard boiled eggs, scrambled egg patties and shrimp. Some foods may retain more nutrients because they are frozen shortly after being harvested. A Stanford University study showed that frozen spinach has 212% more Vitamin C than fresh. Frozen brussels sprouts had 27% more vitamin C than fresh.

QUALITY OF THE FOODS PROCESSED

FRUITS AND VEGETABLES   May be affected by genetic differences, climatic conditions, maturity at harvest or soil differences.

MEAT AND POULTRY   The lowest quality is usually used for canned goods and frozen foods, especially T.V. dinners.

ENRICHMENT AND FORTIFICATION

REFINING OUT AND REPLACING NUTRIENTS   Bread is a good example. Vitamins and minerals are processed out and few are replaced.

FORTIFICATION   Vitamin D is added to milk. Almost all breakfast cereals are fortified, and Vitamin C is added to numerous products.

NOTE: During processing more Vitamin E is lost than any other vitamin. Wheat flour (not the 100% whole wheat flours) loses up to 90% of its Vitamin E value. Rice cereal products may lose up to 70% of their Vitamin E.

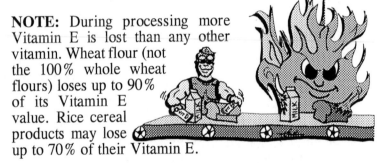

STORAGE OF FOODS

SUPERMARKETS

CANNED AND PACKAGED PRODUCTS   Length of time on the shelf as well as warehouse time results in reduced potencies of vitamins and minerals.

31

FRUITS AND VEGETABLES   Harvested before fully ripened then allowed to ripen in the market. Fruits and vegetables, when cut into smaller sizes are exposed to the effects of light, and air oxidation occurs after long periods without refrigeration.

AT HOME

ROTATION OF FOODS   Canned, frozen, and packaged products are rarely dated and rotated properly. Dehydrated foods as well as restored foods do lose a percentage of their nutrient potency over a period of time and should be utilized before to old.

COMMERCIAL FOOD PRODUCERS

WAREHOUSING   Storage times and temperature changes affect retention of nutrient potencies.

GOVERNMENT WAREHOUSES

CANNED AND PACKAGED FOODS   Storage times usually exceed all other types of storage facilities. Temperature changes are important.

RESTAURANTS

PURCHASING   Restaurants purchase in large quantities, possibly resulting in long storage times, especially if the restaurant is not too busy. Fast food chains avoid this problem due to more frequent food turnover.

NOTE: Excess storage times may result in the purchase of foods thought to contain adequate amounts of certain nutrients which end up with little or none. Oranges from supermarkets have been tested and found to contain no Vitamin C content, while a fresh picked one contains approximately 180mg. Vitamin and mineral potency losses may occur before the product receives its expiration code date. A potato in storage for a period of six months can lose approximately 50% of its Vitamin C content. Most food charts will deduct 25% of the nutrient value of foods to allow for storage, packaging, transportation, processing, preservation, and cooking. In some cases this is not nearly enough.

KNOW YOUR SUPPLEMENT COMPANY

The following steps should be adhered to, to assure quality control by a supplement company. Purchasing discounted products usually means giving up many of these procedures.

1. The manufacturer should store raw materials and bottle them away from heat, light and high moisture areas.

2. Product should be packaged immediately after manufacture.

3. Rotate the inventories to assure fresh product.

4. Product should be manufactured in dehumidified rooms to reduce the effects of moisture.

5. Product should be packaged in containers that do not affect the potency of the product.

6. Utilizing the "state of the art" direct compression methods reduces damage from moisture, heat and light.

7. Purchasing controls should allow raw materials to be used as soon as they arrive.

8. Buying the highest quality raw materials from the finest source.

9. Laboratory-testing all raw materials at regular intervals to assure potency and quality.

10. Natural colors should be used to prevent light from damaging sensitive nutrients.

11. Adding natural fillers and binders as needed.

12. Isolating and granulating certain nutrients to ensure that the sizes will be uniform in relation to the overall product.

13. Performing laboratory testing to ensure that the product will be broken down and the supplement released properly.

14. Using containers that reduce the losses of potency by heat, light and moisture.

15. Periodic laboratory testing to assure that the product retains its potency for a reasonable shelf life.

16. Having independent laboratory tests performed at regular intervals.

Many products may lose up to 50% of their potency after a shelf life of only 6 months.

NUTRIENT DEPLETED SOIL

SOIL PROBLEM

FERTILIZERS   Farmers normally only replace the minerals that are crucial to crop growth, such as phosphorus, potassium and the nitrates.

TRACE MINERALS   The selenium content in soils may vary by a factor of 200 in the United States. A kilogram of wheat may contain from 50mcg to 800mcg of selenium depending where it is grown. Chromium and zinc are also critically deficient in the soil. This problem is presently under extensive study by the Department of Agriculture.

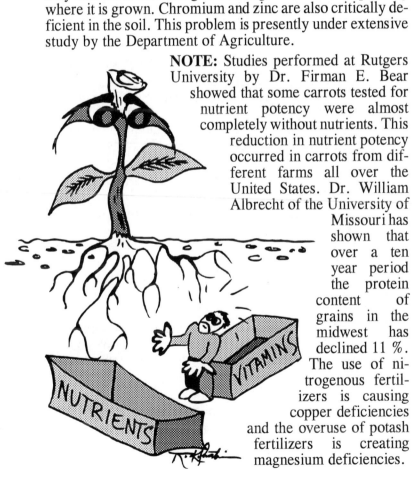

NOTE: Studies performed at Rutgers University by Dr. Firman E. Bear showed that some carrots tested for nutrient potency were almost completely without nutrients. This reduction in nutrient potency occurred in carrots from different farms all over the United States. Dr. William Albrecht of the University of Missouri has shown that over a ten year period the protein content of grains in the midwest has declined 11 %. The use of nitrogenous fertilizers is causing copper deficiencies and the overuse of potash fertilizers is creating magnesium deficiencies.

FOOD ADDITIVES

FLAVORINGS   There are approximately 1100 to 1400 natural and synthetic flavorings available. Scientists are most concerned regarding the toxicity of many of the flavorings. Flavorings make food taste better, restore flavor lost in their processing and can improve natural flavors.

STABILIZERS/JELLING AGENTS/THICKENERS   These are used to keep products such as jellies, jams and baby foods in a "set-state". They are also used to keep ice cream creamy. They generally improve consistency and will affect the appearance and texture of foods. The more common ones are modified food starch and vegetable gums.

COLORINGS   Ninety percent are artificial and have no nutritional value. Some foods have a tendency to lose their natural color when processed and must be dyed back to make them more appealing to the consumer. An example of this is banana ice cream which is dyed yellow. Cherries are almost always dyed.

SWEETENERS   The United States consumption of artificial sweeteners is estimated at approximately six pounds per person per year. These are designed to make the foods more palatable.

AROMA ENHANCERS   An example is the yellowish-green liquid diacetyl which is used in some cottage cheeses to produce an artificial butter aroma.

36

PRESERVATIVES   They help maintain freshness and prevent spoilage that is caused by fungi, yeast, molds and bacteria. Extend shelf life or protect the natural color or flavors.

ACIDS/BASES ALKALIS
Provide a tart flavor for many fruit products, is used for pickling and makes beverages "fizz" using phosphoric acid.

ANTIOXIDANTS   Reduce the possibility of rancidity in fats and oils. Common natural ones are Vitamins C, E and flower pollen. Artificial ones are BHA and BHT.

TASTE ENHANCERS   Brings out the flavor of certain foods. MSG (monosodium glutamate) is a good example.

IMPROVING AGENTS   Examples include humectants - which control the humidity of a food; anti-caking agents - which keep salt and powders free flowing; firming and crisping agents used for processed fruits and vegetables; foaming agents for whipped toppings; anti-foaming agents which keep pineapple juice from bubbling over a filled container.

EMULSIFIERS   These help evenly mix small particles of one liquid with another, such as water and oil. Lecithin is a good example.

NOTE: Keep in mind that you are rarely aware of the quantity of additives you consume. Almost all of these additives require vitamins and minerals to help break them down so that they can be disposed of properly. You may be taking those nutrients away from someplace else that needs them more.

POORLY BALANCED MEALS

MEAL PLANNING   Too few people plan their meals in advance. This results in poor combinations of foods, leading to inadequate vitamin and mineral intake. Lack of nutrition education also plays an important role.

RESTAURANTS   The majority of these meals are lacking in fruits and vegetables.

SUGAR INTAKE

MULTI-FACETED PROBLEM

Sugar requires B vitamins and minerals to enable the body to metabolize it into glucose, yet it contains none of these. Therefore, it must take the nutrients away from other body functions that may need them.

Sugar may also increase the rate at which we excrete the mineral calcium, 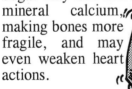 making bones more fragile, and may even weaken heart actions.

Oxalate, contained in chocolate, unites with calcium, carrying it through the intestines as an insoluble compound.

Theobromine in chocolate may reduce the absorption of protein through the intestinal wall.

38

NOTE: High sugar intake reduces the effectiveness of the body's healing mechanism, causing a prolongation in the healing time.

SMOKING

EFFECTS ON VITAMINS

VITAMIN C   Studies have shown that smokers require approximately 40% more Vitamin C intake than non-smokers to achieve adequate blood levels. Every cigarette reduces bodily stores of Vitamin C by approximately 30mg, which means a pack of cigarettes requires at least a 600mg increase in your Vitamin C intake.

Vitamin B12   Cigarette smoking reduces the blood levels of Vitamin B12.

COOKING/FOOD PREPARATION

PREPARATION OF FOODS

WASHING/SOAKING   Many vitamins are water-soluble and will be lost through washing, scrubbing or long periods of soaking. Soaking carrots causes the loss of the natural sugar, all the B vitamins, Vitamins C and D, and all minerals except calcium.

DICING/SLICING/PEELING/SHREDDING   The smaller you cut fruit and vegetables the more surface is exposed to temperature changes, air oxidation, and light. Prepare as close to serving time as possible.

Shredding for salads causes a 20% loss of Vitamin C and an additional 20% loss if the salad stands for an hour before eating it.

NOTE: The skin of fruits and vegetables contains at least 10% of the nutritional content of that food.

METHODS OF COOKING

CHARCOAL   Pyrobenzines may be produced by the fat dripping on the charcoal. These chemical substances are classified as carcinogens (cancer forming agents).

CROCK-POT   Vegetables left in all day or for a long period of time lose a high percentage of their vitamins and minerals, as well as absorbing the fat from the meats. Steam vegetables first and then add them to the pot before serving.

BOILING   Stewing and boiling fruits and vegetables results in heavy nutrient losses.

STEAMING   This is by far the best method for preparing fruits and vegetables. They are subjected to high temperatures for only a short period of time.

MICROWAVE   Very good method. Foods cook fast and have
    less chance of loosing their nutrients.

FRYING   High heat causes nutrient losses in all types of foods.
    Meats will lose Vitamin B1 and pantothenic acid.

   NOTE: Refrigerate all foods as soon as possible; this will
   help you retain the potencies of the vitamins and minerals.
   Whole boiled carrots will retain 90% of their Vitamin C
   and most of their minerals, but if you slice them up before
   cooking you will lose almost all the Vitamin C and niacin
   content.

AIR POLLUTION

SMOG   All major cities in the Unites States have some form of
    chemical air pollution. This pollution will effect your lungs'
    capacity to deliver oxygen efficiently to the cells of the
    body. The antioxidants, Vitamins A, C,
    E, selenium and flower pollen have
    proved to be effective in
    combating some of the
    effect of smog.

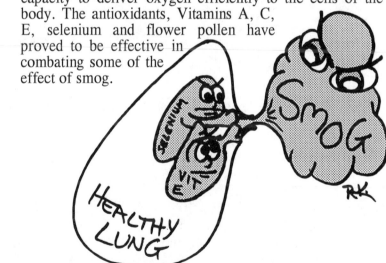

SMOKE   The smoke from cigarettes, cigars and pipes all has a
    detrimental effect on the oxygen carrying capacity of the red
    blood cells. Smoke contains carbon monoxide which may
    adhere to the site on the red blood cell that should be carry-
    ing oxygen.

41

THE AGING PROCESS

NUTRIENT REQUIREMENTS CHANGE WITH AGE

DAIRY PRODUCT INTOLERANCE   The enzyme to break down lactase has the tendency to be reduced in its effectiveness as we age. May lead to reduction of calcium intake.

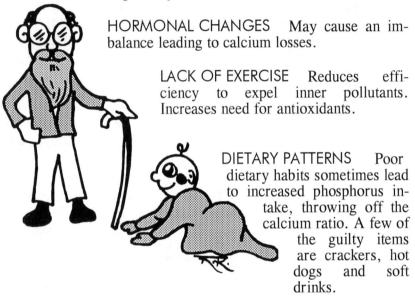

HORMONAL CHANGES   May cause an imbalance leading to calcium losses.

LACK OF EXERCISE   Reduces efficiency to expel inner pollutants. Increases need for antioxidants.

DIETARY PATTERNS   Poor dietary habits sometimes lead to increased phosphorus intake, throwing off the calcium ratio. A few of the guilty items are crackers, hot dogs and soft drinks.

SENILITY   Some symptoms may be caused by a lack of Vitamin B6 in the diet.

CIRCULATION PROBLEMS   Tissues receive poor oxygenation. Antioxidants may help improve the utilization of available oxygen.

IMMUNE SYSTEM   Antioxidants may reduce cellular degeneration, thus increasing the effectiveness of the system. Prostate problems, depending on the problem, may respond to zinc supplement or flower pollen.

NOTE: Vitamin E prolongs the life of red blood cells by reducing the formation of toxic peroxides, which some scientists feel may speed up the aging process.

42

STRESS

VITAMIN B   The health of nerves and especially their protective sheath depends on an adequate supply of Vitamin B.

SUGAR AND ALCOHOL Both require Vitamin B for their breakdown. Excess amounts in the system cause a shortage of available Vitamin B.

VITAMIN C   Bodily needs for Vitamin C may increase as much as 100 times when we are under stress.

ILLNESSES/DISEASES

ASTHMA   The degree of exercise induced bronchospasm may be reduced if the person takes approximately 500mg of Vitamin C six hours or less before the exercise.

HYPERACTIVITY   Cause may be linked to Vitamin B deficiency due to over-consumption of refined carbohydrates, mainly sugars.

CIRCULATORY PROBLEMS   Respond well to Vitamin E and other antioxidants.

VARICOSE VEINS   Respond well to Vitamin E therapy in a high percentage of cases.

UNEXPLAINED BRUISES Vitamin C therapy is being utilized in some cases and has shown to be effective.

DIETING

Weight management programs should contain the following components:

1. A variety of meal replacement foods.

2. No less than 900 calories per day.

3. Behavior modification information and follow-up.

4. One well balanced meal per day.

5. A quality vitamin and mineral supplement.

ENDLESS PROGRAMS

Because of the multitude of diet programs available on the market, it is impossible to list the nutritional inadequacies found in most programs. These programs do not take into consideration the individual life-style differences in the persons using the products. In many cases these products are abused to a dangerous point.

BELLY HOLDER

PULL OUT SHELF

ALCOHOL ABUSE

VITAMIN AND MINERAL NEEDS   To be broken down by the body, alcohol requires numerous B vitamin and minerals. B Vitamins include thiamine, riboflavin, niacin, pantothenic acid and biotin. Minerals include iron, zinc, manganese, magnesium, phosphorus and copper .

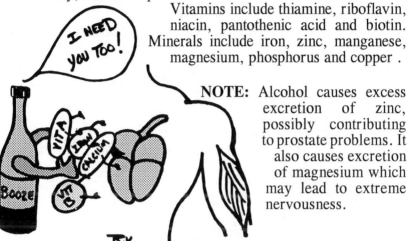

NOTE: Alcohol causes excess excretion of zinc, possibly contributing to prostate problems. It also causes excretion of magnesium which may lead to extreme nervousness.

EXERCISE

ANTIOXIDANTS   Increase the oxygen utilization by the body. Promote efficient use of available oxygen. Vitamin E, flower pollen and selenium are very effective.

BIRTH CONTROL PILLS

HORMONE EFFECTS   Because of the estrogen content in oral contraceptives, studies have shown that women on the Pill have lower than normal blood serum levels of Vitamin B6 and Vitamin C. Daily supplementation should be 50mg to

45

75mg of B6 and 1000mg to 2000mg of Vitamin C. A time release C would be best.

RESTAURANTS

FOOD PREPARATION

Additional destruction of nutrients is caused by exposure of food to air, light, and continual heating until served.

HEART DISEASE ---- ATHEROSCLEROSIS

CHELATION   Involves the use of various vitamins and minerals to aide in clearing deposits (plaque) in the walls of arteries. Certain nutrients adhere to specific heavy metals and carry them out of the body. A quality chelated mineral is best.

ANTIOXIDANTS   Available oxygen must be utilized to the fullest degree when arteries are partially blocked.

LECITHIN   Binds fats so that they will more easily be cleared from the body. Vitamin B6 helps the body process a toxic substance, "homocysteine", into a safe compound. Excess amounts of this compound have been related to an increase in atherosclerosis.

CANCER

CELL GROWTH   Numerous studies have provided sufficient evidence that the antioxidants, vitamins A, C, E, selenium and flower pollen may reduce the risk of cancer and even provide some relief after it is contracted. The growth of cancer cells are slowed in the presence of higher amounts of oxygen. The more oxygen your cells have access to, the better.

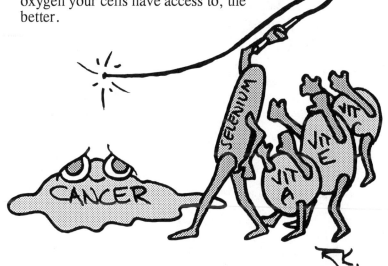

VITAMIN - ANTAGONIST RELATIONSHIPS

VITAMIN	ANTAGONIST
Vitamin A	Mineral Oil, Air Pollution/Smog, Fertilizer Nitrates
Vitamin D	Anti-Convulsive Drugs, Mineral Oil
Thiamine B1	Antibiotics, Excess Heat cooking, etc., Sugar Consumption, Alcohol, Stress Situations
Riboflavin B2	Antibiotics, Exposure to Light, Excess Heat, Alcohol, Oral Contraceptives
Niacin	Antibiotics, Sugars Consumption, Excess Heat, Alcohol, Intestinal Absorption Reduced During Illnesses
Pantothenic Acid B5	Methyl Bromide insecticide fumigant for foods
Pyridoxine B6	Aging levels decline after 50, Steroid Hormones estrogen, etc., Hydralazine hypertension drug, Excess Heat, Food Processing
Folic Acid	Oral Contraceptives, Stress Situations, Vitamin C Deficiency
Vitamin B12	Prolonged Iron Deficiency, Stress Situations, Oral Contraceptives
Biotin	Excess Heat, Antibiotics, Sulfa Drugs, Avidin in raw egg whites
Choline	Sugar Consumption, Alcohol
Inositol	Antibiotics when intestinal bacteria is destroyed
Vitamin C	Overexertion fatigue, Stress Situations, Aspirin, Smoking, Alcohol, Corticosteroids
Vitamin E	Oral Contraceptives, Food Processing, Rancid Fats and Oils, Mineral Oil
Vitamin K	Antibiotics, Mineral Oil, Radiation, Anticoagulants

NITRATES AND NITRITES

VITAMIN RELATIONSHIP

VITAMIN C   If Vitamin C is not present when these chemicals are ingested they may combine with an amino acid to form "nitrosamines." Nitrosamines are carcinogens or cancer producing agents, and studies show they cause cancerous tumors in laboratory animals. This group of chemicals is found in all processed meats, for example; hot dogs and lunch meat.

BIOFLAVONOID VITAMIN P

GENERAL INFORMATION

SOURCE   Citrus fruit skin and pulp, green peppers, apricots, cherries, tomatoes, papaya, grapes, broccoli and cantaloupe.

BENEFITS   Strengthens small blood vessels and capillaries. Decreases capillary fragility and prevents pressure problems. Protects against abnormal uterine bleeding. Alleviates hemorrhoid and varicose vein problems.

NOTE: In cases where Vitamin C is not effective, it becomes effective when bioflavonoids are added. Laboratory produced "synthetic" Vitamin C does not contain bioflavonoid. This is a good reason to purchase "natural" Vitamin C.

POLYUNSATURATED FATTY ACIDS (PUFA)

TWO TYPES

CIS-FORM FATTY ACIDS   A horseshoe shaped molecule of PUFA that occurs naturally in nature and is normally incorporated into a healthy cell wall. The health of the cell wall is dependent on a supply of cis-form fatty acids. When these

49

acids are not available the cell wall is constructed with abnormal openings ports of entry that may allow foreign substances to enter and cause problems.

TRANS-FORM FATTY ACIDS   Instead of the normal horseshoe form, the trans-form fatty acids are found in a straight line shape. This form of the acid is difficult for the cell to utilize when constructing a new cell wall. The blueprint calls for a horseshoe shape, not the straight line shape. Trans fatty acids are formed by the refining, deodorizing, hydrogenating and cooking of fats and oils. Processing alone results in trans-acids being present in fresh store bought products such as pure liquid oil containing up to 6% trans fatty acids, margarines up to 54%, and shortenings up to 58%. Heating and storage of these fats and oils then increases this percentage.

NOTE: Trans fatty acids can be identified by the term "partially hydrogenated vegetable oil" on the list of ingredients of commercially-prepared products. Avoidance of products containing trans-form fatty acids is almost impossible. Vitamin E provides a measure of protection against the formation of trans-form fatty acids.

WATER

VARIOUS TYPES

TAP WATER   Chlorine uses up Vitamin E stored in the body.

BOTTLED WATER   Good water to use without added chlorine.

SOFT WATER   Removes calcium and magnesium and adds sodium. Not recommended for drinking.

DISTILLED WATER   Safest water for drinking. Obtain your minerals through proper diet and a quality food supplement.

SYNTHETIC vs. NATURAL

Unfortunately the confusion over the terms "natural" and "synthetic" continues, with little relief in sight.

The articles and studies are numerous with the predominant facts still leaning toward the "natural" side by a wide margin.

A synthetic vitamin is one that is produced in a laboratory by constructing a chemical compound with the exact molecular structure of a particular vitamin. It contains no enzymes, co-enzymes, minerals, mineral activators or other related elements that work synergistically with that vitamin. An example is "natural" Vitamin C which contains in its natural state bioflavonoid found in the skins of fruit and aids in the proper assimilation of the vitamin. This is not found in synthetic Vitamin C (ascorbic acid). A noted allergist, Dr. Theron Randolph, says, "A synthetically derived substance may cause a reaction in a chemically susceptible person, when the same material of natural origin is tolerated, despite the two substances having identical chemical structures."

The average person with limited knowledge in the field of nutrition does not know which way to turn. Should they sacrifice the "natural" for the lower-priced "synthetic" or pay the extra money and possibly obtain a higher quality product? When it comes to deciding on the purchase of a "natural" over a "synthetic" I feel we should listen to what a few of the experts say. Earl Mindell, author of "The Vitamin Bible," goes into extensive detail on vitamins and their individual attributes. He explains, "though synthetic vitamins and minerals have produced satisfactory results, the benefits from natural vitamins, on a variety of levels, surpass them." Dr. Clive McCoy, Director of Nutrition Research at Cornell University, gives us eight rules for proper nutrition. His fifth rule states "instead of synthetic vitamins, use natural vitamins." Dr. Jeffrey Bland, professor of chemistry at the University of Puget Sound, after comparing the activity of "natural"d-form Vitamin E and "synthetic" dl-form Vitamin E found that the synthetic form had less than 30% of the activity of the natural form. He also found that the synthetic form inhibited the natural form from entering the cellular membrane.

> **NOTE:** An all-natural vitamin must state that all ingredients are from natural sources.

WHY CHELATED MINERALS?

The word "chelate" is derived from the Greek word "chele" which means claw. Originally it referred to the clamping down of a crab's claw. Its relationship to chelated minerals refers to the action of one or more amino acid proteins attaching itself and completely surrounding a mineral, with a new complex being formed in this protective coating. The quality of this coating varies from product to product and that old saying, "you get what you pay for," is very true.

When ingesting a tablet or capsule of a commercially prepared chelated mineral product, the initial environment it comes into contact with is stomach acid. In this acidic medium poorly coated capsules and tablets may fall completely apart. Capsules disintegrate in approximately two minutes, with tablets lasting about fifteen minutes.

The stomach acid then breaks down the chelate coating and ionizes the mineral, allowing it to go free to react with anything it comes into contact with. Any chelate that might have been formed around the mineral is now gone. This is why it is essential for chelates to be made from amino acids using milk solids as the source and not amino acids made from incomplete vegetable proteins.

Incomplete vegetable proteins have the tendency to allow the stomach acid to remove and actually tear apart the chelate material. When this occurs the mineral may reach the intestines, form an insoluble precipitate and be excreted.

If, however, a quality chelate coating is applied, the mineral is protected by this pH sensitive coating and reaches the intestines where the coating should dissolve, allowing absorption of the mineral and utilization by the body. Chelated minerals may therefore be considered safer, mainly because they can be taken in smaller amounts instead of a larger, possibly toxic dose to acheive the desired level.

DISEASES AND CONDITIONS THAT CAN BE PREVENTED BY IMPROVED NUTRITION

HEALTH PROBLEM	POTENTIAL SAVINGS
1. Cardiovascular System	25 Percent Reduction
2. Respiratory Disease	20 Percent Fewer Incidents
3. Mental Health	10 Percent Fewer Disabilities
4. Infant Mortality	50 Percent Fewer Deaths
5. Early Aging and Lifespan	10 Million People without Impairments
6. Arthritis	8 Million People relieved of Afflictions
7. Dental Health	50 Percent Reduction of Problems
8. Diabetes	50 Percent Cases Avoided
9. Osteoporosis	75 Percent Reduction
10. Obesity	80 Percent Reduction in Incidence
11. Alcoholism	33 Percent Reduction
12. Eyesight	20 Percent Reduction Wearing Corrective Lenses
13. Allergies	20 Percent People Relieved
14. Digestive	25 Percent Fewer Conditions
15. Kidney and Urinary	20 Percent Reduction
16. Muscular Disorders	10 Percent Reduction in Cases
17. Cancer	20 Percent Reduction in Incidence and death
18. Improved Work Efficiency	0.5 Percent Increase in Productivity
19. Improved Learning Ability	10 Point I.Q. Raise of Persons with I.Q. of 70-80
20. Carbohydrate Disorders	50 Percent Improved

PHYTOCHEMICALS — NEW KID ON THE BLOCK

Simply put, these are not nutrients, not vitamins, not minerals, just chemical compounds that exist in fruits and vegetables. They have been known for years, but never received much press or attention until recent studies started linking them to cancer prevention in laboratory animals.

Studies on phytochemicals are presently being conducted by numerous agencies and universities including The National Cancer Society and National Academy of Science.

One very important factor is that phytochemicals are not destroyed by cooking or processing to any great degree. There are over 100,000 phytochemicals. The following are a few of the more important ones:

PHYTOCHEMICALS IN FRUIT AND VEGETABLES

There could be as many as 100,000 different phytochemicals

	FOOD	PHYTOCHEMICAL
	Broccoli Cauliflower, Brussell Sprouts, Kale, Etc.	SULFORAPHANE Activates enzyme that aids in removing carcinogens from body
		DITHIOLTHIONES Triggers production of enzymes that may block carcinogens from damaging DNA
	Sweet Potatoes Yams	FLAVONOIDS Attached to cancer cells and stops hormones from attaching

PHYTOCHEMICALS IN FRUIT AND VEGETABLES

Cabbage, Turnips Turnips, Etc.	**INDOLES** Studies show that they reduce the risks of breasts cancer
	PHENETHYL ISOTHIOCYANATE Has a disarming effect on cancer cells

Soybeans Dried Beans Mung Bean Sprouts	**GENISTEIN** Cuts off blood supply by retarding their capillary growth
Chili Peppers	**CAPSAICIN** Stops toxic molecules from attaching to DNA

Citrus Fruit	**LIMONENE** Activates enzyme that disposes of carcinogens
Apples/Fruits	**CAFFEIC ACID** Increases the solubility of toxins in water so that they will flush out of the body
	FERULIC ACID Binds to nitrates in stomach

Grapes Strawberries Raspberries	**ELLAGIC ACID** May prevent carcinogens from entering DNA
Garlic Onions Leeks	**ALLYLIC SULFIDE** Detoxifies carcinogens

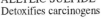

Chives	**ALLIUM COMPOUNDS** Slows reproduction of carcinogens, allows more time for them to be destroyed
Grains	PHYTIC ACID Binds to iron, thus reducing a free radical production mechanism

Tomatoes Green Peppers	P-COUMARIC & CHLORGENIC ACIDS Kills cancer forming substances in their formation stages This group contains over 10,000 phytochemicals

OPTIMUM HEALTH —IS IT POSSIBLE?

Optimum health requires that all of the body's biologic systems must be in a state of "homeostasis" balance with all environmental stressors. Many diseases, in fact 70% of all illnesses may be environmentally triggered, which simply means that we are causing many of our own diseases ourselves.

There is an important point to remember that all physicians are aware of; it is called the "rule of 60%." This simply means that in most disease states the system or organ involved will not show any sign of a clinical symptom until the system or organ has reached a state of deterioration of 60% or more. In many cases it is then too late to do anything to reverse the problem.

PREVENTION —INSTEAD OF INTERVENTION

The body is very adaptive and will use a poorer quality component or nutrient to complete a process; it has no choice if that's all you give it to use. The body is very adaptive and a good example of that is in the following:

ADAPTIVE STATE REGARDING TOBACCO

1. First time smoker: body tries to tell you it doesn't like it and produces symptoms such as dizziness, sick to your stomach, headaches, etc.

2. You insist that you will smoke: body says OK, I need to survive this and compensates.

3. Body uses energy to maintain a poor level of health. Cells now have to function in a sea of toxins.

4. Eventually, leads to poorer health and disease and then premature death.

TO ACHIEVE OPTIMUM HEALTH

MENTALLY FIT   In control of body, not body in control of you.

METABOLICALLY FIT   Eat the right foods, low-fat diet.

SUPPLEMENTALLY FIT   Consume balanced formulations and a quality antioxidant.

PROPORTIONALLY FIT   Your weight should match your build and never be more than 8-10 pounds over your ideal weight.

PHYSICALLY FIT   Exercise regularly.

ANTIOXIDANT CELLULAR EFFICIENCY TEST

by Myles H. Bader, Dr.PH, MPH

This test is designed to evaluate the numerous factors that reduce the effectiveness of antioxidants. Since the fight between antioxidant protection and free-radical damage occurs in a thousandths of a second, the antioxidant bioavailability must be instantly ready to safely neutralize the free radical.

Your awareness of nutritional and environmental factors and your ability to control these factors will determine whether your body will be able to achieve an optimum level of health or just satisfactorily function until a breakdown occurs or disease process obtains a foothold.

The following test does not relate in any way to a prediction or diagnosis of your antioxidant status, but is for educational purposes only.

If a question does not apply, do not answer it. Start with the figure 100, then add or subtract as you answer the questions.

Please turn to the next page for your ACE Test.

Antioxidant Cellular Efficiency Test (ACE)

I Lifestyle Factors That Reduce Bioavailability of Antioxidants

	Often	Seldom	Never	Score
I exercise in a smoggy area	-4	-9	0	
I use tobacco (smoking or chewing)	-20	-9	0	
I am exposed to second hand smoke	-8	-3	0	
Air pollution is a factor where I live/ work	-5	-3	0	
Exposure to sunlight	-10	-5	0	
Consume more than 2 alcoholic beverages per day	-25	-8	0	
Take prescription drugs regularly	-10	-8	0	
Restricted caloric dieting	-25	-10	0	
Take oral contraceptive	-10	NA	0	
Eat fried foods more than 3 times per week	-12	-7	0	
Function as a Type A personality	-22	-10	0	
Regularly constipated	-27	-12	0	

II Nutritional Variables

	Often	Seldom	Never	Score
Consume at least 4-5 serving of fruits and vegetables daily	+26	+10	-26	
Consume 3 servings of whole grains or legumes daily	+15	+6	-15	
Consume at least 1 serving of broccoli, cauliflower, kale or brussel sprouts daily	+10	+3	-30	
Eat no more that 15-20% fat as total calories	+30	+18	-30	
Eat fish 3-4 times per week	+10	+4	-8	
Drink 6-8 glasses of water daily	+10	+4	-12	

III Significant Health Factors That May Increase Antioxidant Needs

Answer the following questions as they relate to your health over the last 12 months

	Severe	Moderate	Mild	Often	Seldom	Never	Score
Diabetes	-27	-15				0	
High cholesterol/lipids	>250. -30	<250. -20	good <200. +15				
Respiratory problems	-25	-15	-8				
Coronary artery disease	-40	-30	-20				

	Severe	Moderate	Mild	Often	Seldom	Never	Score
Frequent illness or infections		-25		-18	-10	+20	
Digestive problems				-14	-5	+16	
Gum bleeding				-6	-2	+8	
Easily stressed				-18	-10	+20	
Chemotherapy or radiation	-30	-20	-10				

IV   Present Supplement Intake

			Often	Seldom	Never	
Take a multi-vitamin			+8	+2	-8	
Vitamin C supplement			+8	+2	-8	
Antioxidant Formula			+25	+10	-25	
Chelated Multi-mineral			+8	+2	-8	

HEALTH EXPECTANCY RESULTS

To calculate your antioxidant Cellular Efficiency Index Score, do the following:

Enter your final score (starting with +100)	
Add 40	
Subtract Your Age	
Final Total	

RATING CHART

90 or higher	**Excellent Antioxidant Levels**
80-89	**Very Good**
65-79	**Good**
50-64	**Fair**
30-49	**Poor Status**
1-29	**Hope You Have Good Heredity**
Minus Score	**Need Immediate Intervention**

RESOURCES

Cancer and Vitamin C: Cameron, Ewan & Pauling, Linus, Warner, NY

You Can Fight for Your Life: LeShan, Lawrence, M. Evans & Co., NY, NY

Anatomy Of An Illness: Cousins, Norman, Bantam, NY

Freedom From Stress, A Holistic Approach: Nuernberger, Phil, Honesdale, PA

Nutrient To Age Without Senility: Hoffer, Abram & Walker, Morton, Keats, New Canaan, Conn.

The Justification For Vitamin Supplementation: Bland, Jeffery, Northwest Diagnostics, Bellevue, WA

Nutrition Against Disease: Williams, Roger, J., Pitman Publ., NY.

Diet & Disease: Cheraskin, Emanuel & Ringsdorf, W.M. & Clark, J.W., Keats Publ., New Canaan, Conn.

Nutrition & Vitamin Therapy: Lesser, Michael, Bantam, NY

Sweet And Dangerous: Yudkin, John, Bantam, NY

Vitamin Bible: Mindell, Earl, Warner, NY

Journal of the American Medical Association

Annals of Allergy

Arizona Medicine: 16:100

British Journal of Nutrition: 26,89

American Journal of Clinical Nutrition

Dairy Council Digest

Family Health

Consumers Digest

Modern Medicine

Nutrition and Therapeutics: Vol. 11, No. 4.

Prepared Foods

Roche Chemical, Food Department: Nutley, NJ

Proctor & Schwartz Inc., Dehydrated Foods: Glascow, Scotland

Environmental Nutrition Newsletter

Prevention

Journal of Nutrition for the Elderly

Research on Nutrition, Aging and Immunity: Concord, CA

American Journal of Clinical Nutrition

Cancer: 47:1226-1240

Lancet

Rx Being Well

Nutrition in Medical Practice: Philadelphia: Saunders

The Living State: NY: Academic Press

Annals of the New York Academy of Science

Family Practice News

Current Therapeutic Research

Science Newsletter

Lancet

Feed Age

SPECIAL STUDIES
Judy Brown PhD., Dept. of Nutrition, Univ. of Minnesota. *Oral Contraceptives* Dr. Alfred Knudson, Philadelphia's Fox Chase Cancer Center. *Cancer* Dr. Daniel Medina, Baylor College of Medicine. *Cancer* Dr. Roy L. Walford, U.C.L.A. *Aging* Dr. Howard Lutz, Institute for Preventive Medicine, Washington, DC. *Stress*

Dr. Myles H. Bader's Formulas to the Rescue!

Certain chemicals, vitamins and minerals act as antioxidants to help the body's own scavengers destroy free radicals. The role of antioxidants is still being studied. However, in all research to date, they are "highly recommended in over 60 diseases as a preventative measure or to reduce the severity of a disease in patients who already show symptoms."

Dr. Myles H. Bader's Formulas declare war on free radicals. A 100% natural product, it can help:
* shield your cells against free radicals,
* dislodge existing free radicals from cellular tissue,
* flush free radicals from your body, and
* stimulate the natural biochemicals in your body to maximize their potential to fight free radicals and rebuild damaged cells.

Dr. Myles H. Bader's Formulas combine, in one potent compound, the most effective antioxidants now known through research: proanthocyanidin, phytochemicals (powdered vegetables), selenium, and vitamins A (Beta Carotene), C and E.

For Further Information
Call:

1-800-717-6001

Three Formulas to meet your needs:

Dr. Myles H. Bader's Enhanced Vitamin Formula 1 with Proanthocyanidin (Canada) and Super Antioxidant Formula 1 (USA), if you are in reasonably good health.

Dr. Myles H. Bader's Enhanced Vitamin Formula 2 with Proanthocyanidin (Canada) and Super Antioxidant Formula 2 (USA), if you are generally tired and need a boost.

Dr. Myles H. Bader's Enhanced Vitamin Formula 3 with Proanthocyanidin (Canada) and Super Antioxidant Formula 3 (USA), if you suffer from health problems.

For Further Information Call:

1-800-717-6001

✦ Northstar Publishing Company ✦

(702) 383-8511 Tel   1818 Industrial Road, Suite 209 Las Vegas, NV 89102   (702) 383-9145 Fax

HOW TO ORDER: Please use this form when ordering. This catalog is mailed to all customers on our active mailing list. To remain on the active mailing list, please place at least one order per year for Dr. Bader's Books.

TELEPHONE ORDERS: For fastest service, order by book number directly from NPC between 8am and 5pm PT, Monday - Friday.

CALL TOLL FREE 1-800-717-6001

FAX ORDERS: To fax your order, please complete this order form and fax it to: 1-702-383- 9828

MAIL ORDERS: Please return this form and your check or purchase order to:

```
YOUR SATISFACTION
GUARANTEED
NPC will promptly refund your payment
for any book returned within 15 days
after you receive it.
```

**Northstar Publishing
1818 Industrial Road
Suite. 209
Las Vegas, NV 89102
1-702-383-8511**

Bookstores and Promotional Buyers: If you are a bookstore or need books for promotional use, call one of our friendly staff who is waiting to help you at:
1-800-717-6001

Qty.	Order No.	Title	Price Ea.	Total
	001	"6001 Food Facts and Chef's Secrets"	18.95	
	002	"Cherry Creations"	15.95	
	003	"To Supplement or Not To Supplement"	5.95	

Check/Money Order $ Enclosed _____

Purchase Order Attached # _____

☐ VISA   ☐ MASTERCARD   ☐ DISCOVER

1 2 3 4 5 6 7 8 9 10 11 12 13 14 15 16

Card Account Number   (Please list all numbers on card)

Subtotal	
NV Sales Tax	
Shp&Hdl*	
Total	

Make Payable in US Dollars

Month   Year   _____ Signature

Expiration Date Required

Address Change, Shipping Address or Mailing List

Name _____

Address _____

City _____ State ___ Zip _____

Daytime phone (___) _____

```
*Shipping & Handling Charges
$3.75 For The First Book U.S.A.
$4.75 For The First Book Canada
$1.75 For Each Additional Book
Books are mailed Book Rate via
the US Post Office unless
otherwise requested.
```

NOTES

NOTES

NOTES

NOTES